# The Cascade Effect

"Faith and knowledge lean largely upon each other
in the practice of medicine."

- Peter Mere Latham -

# The Cascade Effect

A Biologist Shares His Faith
and His Story Living with
Wilson's Disease (An inherited
disorder of copper metabolism)

W. Mark Dendy

Cover Illustration copyright © 2010 by JoAnne Rosenfeld
Cover layout by Eveline Fisher, Jennifer Moore, and Margaret Souliere
Editing by Alison Loscotoff


Printed in the United States of America

First Printing, 2010

ISBN-10: 1-4515-4705-6
ISBN-13: 978-1-4515-4705-4

WMD Books
P.O. Box 1551
Elk Grove, CA 95759

www.WMDBooks.com

For my loving wife, Zeta
Our three children, Steven, A.J. and Lyndsie
My sister, JoAnne
(who designed the cover)
my sister, Cathy
and the one who gave birth to me,
my mom, Aileen V. Dendy
(carrier of the defective copper transport gene)

And in loving memory of my dear father,
Wallace Lafayette Dendy May 5, 1922 – March 19, 1991
(the other carrier of the defective copper transport gene)

# About the Cover

The cover was designed by my oldest sister, JoAnne Rosenfeld. The cascading pennies are symbolic of the effects that result from my body's inability to metabolize copper. Using her artistic and creative talents, JoAnne dated the pennies with significant dates: 1954 – the year I was born; 1982 – the year I was diagnosed with Wilson's disease; and 2010 – the year of my story's publication.

JoAnne was born and raised in Mississippi. She is a self-taught artist who began copying comics out of the Sunday paper at age four, and as a high school senior, she won first, second, and third prize in a statewide poster contest. After high school, she exhibited in many venues, such as museums, libraries, and banks; she also sold at art shows.

JoAnne resides in Egg Harbor with her husband Jeff Rosenfeld, where they both enjoy the retired life.

I am happy to call JoAnne my sister, and happy to say that she did not inherit Wilson's disease!

# Contents

# Foreword

Wilson's disease, similar to many other genetic diseases, is determined by a small gene mutation. This anomaly is responsible for the accumulation of an enormous amount of toxic copper in the body with consequences mainly for the liver and the brain. A person's life will always be influenced by this little mistake of nature. But the story does not end here: a life with Wilson's disease can be as full as any life. Full of successes and struggles, full of happiness and sadness, full of love and achievements, as well as, surprises and unexpected turns. Wilson disease is one of the few examples of genetic diseases where the medical therapy can guarantee a normal life if the diagnosis is made early in the disease progression. In my experience with Wilson disease, both in Europe and in the United States, I have witnessed amazing stories of life and hope, all characterized by patients eager to live their lives without any limitations and caring doctors willing to explore all possibilities to help them. Nevertheless, it is still an orphan disease, and every effort to increase awareness of this condition and its treatment options is very important. Our knowledge is still very limited in regards to some of the disease manifestations. Psychiatric symptoms often remain untreated or improperly managed.

This often leads to frustration, disappointment, and sadness for both patients and doctors.

The author, Mark Dendy, has been very generous to share his personal story with all of us. He has the intent to expand the knowledge and hopefully provide information and insights for new scientific discoveries of Wilson disease. His efforts to make public his suffering through his life, and his striving to have a proactive role in the management of his condition will be an inspiration for other patients as well as for physicians and scientists.

Valentina Medici, M.D.
Assistant Professor
University of California, Davis
Division of Gastroenterology &
Hepatology
Department of Internal Medicine

# Acknowledgements

Whatever the weaknesses of this book, they would have been far greater without the kind help of my sister JoAnne for her creative and God given artistic talent, my mother and my sister Cathy and their recollections of dates and events, Eveline Fisher, Jennifer Moore, and Margaret Souliere for their patience with me and expertise in the cover layout, and my editor, Alison Loscotoff with her keen eye for detail and help in bringing life to my story. And I would be amiss if I did not thank my wife, Zeta, Dr. Paul Seites, Dr. Valentina Medici, and Dr. Vicki Wheelock for their constant encouragement to tell my story.

# Introduction
## This is my story!

I began writing this book in my head some years ago. My thoughts are often so scattered; I find myself challenged to remember them or put them in writing. With today's modern technology, I find it easier to tell my story to a microphone and computer, and these are the results after a microprocessor has compiled my thoughts and put them on paper.

On the eve July 24, 1954, my mother and father had played cards at another couple's home. My mother felt tired and a little ill and they returned home early that night. My mother was awakened shortly after midnight, and at 2:30 a.m. Dr. Manning delivered me, a 9 pound 2 1/2 ounce boy.

My mother and father had not planned on me, but they took great pride in their new son and named me William Mark Dendy - William after my father's father and Mark after the apostle and Gospel writer. I appeared to be a healthy and happy baby, and, with the exception of being accident prone, I was healthy for the first 2 1/2 decades of my life.

In 1981, at age 27, I began to experience severe mood changes and developed a tremor in my right hand that went from mild to severe in a matter of weeks. I was dumbfounded, confused, and angry over my rapidly deteriorating health. I had moved back home to Maryland after living for four years in Southern California. The return to my hometown, I later came to realize, was just one of the many instances God was looking after me.

I became a believer at a young age, nine years old to be exact. I accepted Jesus Christ as my personal savior on July 10, 1964, but it wasn't until I became severely ill that I truly recognized God's hand in every waking moment of my life.

You see, I never doubted God's existence, and there was only a brief period in my life where I entertained the God-less concept of evolution. I knew God had created the heavens and the universe, that He was everywhere and could do anything at any time, however, I never recognized Him as my caregiver. Had I searched the Scriptures, I would have known that despite the fact that I didn't give him my all, He still looked after me and sought a relationship with me.

This is my story!

# Chapter 1
## Life or Death

I could see the railroad crossing arms going down 50 yards ahead of me on Elk Grove Boulevard. I was headed to the Union 76 station to fill the propane tank for our grill; we were having a barbeque on that sunny Sunday afternoon in early May, 2008. My wife, daughter, mother and one of my sons were all at the house awaiting my return. We had just been to church that morning and my emotional state was, I would say... pretty good. All of a sudden, this "feeling" came over me...

I was the first car in line before the train tracks and I could see a freight train approaching at a high rate of speed. It was speeding past me at 50 or 60 miles per hour when the thought invaded my mind. All I had to do was take my foot off the brake and hit the accelerator and it would all be over in a split second!

I watched the train speeding past as if in a trance, thinking, "no one else would be hurt." There was nothing between me and that mass of speeding steel... I kept saying to myself, "No one else would get hurt! No one else will get hurt! NO ONE ELSE WILL GET HURT!"

My knees were shaking. I tapped my thumbs on the steering wheel, gripped tightly in my hands as if death were imminent. A voice in my head taunted me, "Go ahead, do it." "It would all be over in a second," the voice whispered, "no more pain, no more medicine to take, no more bitchin' and moanin'... trust me, you will be at peace!"

The train speeding by, the sound of my fingers tapping, the quivering in my legs as I began to lift my foot off the brake, it all seemed amplified as tears welled up in my eyes. What about my wife and kids? My mom and sisters? They would not be able to have an open casket. My body would be shredded by the clash of metal against metal with me in the middle. How would they deal with the anguish? The death of a husband, father, brother, and son might devastate them, WOULD devastate them!

It seemed, in this moment, as though an angel had appeared to thwart off the demon that was tormenting me with these thoughts of taking my own life. I began to think of Flip Wilson and the devil and angel on each shoulder in his television comedy routine. My forehead was resting on the steering wheel between my hands. My fingers were no longer tapping. My legs had found new strength. A horn honked. I sat up and saw that the train had passed… surely, God had sent an angel to save me from my own self destruction again!

* * *

A year and a half later, I met with Dr. Valentini Medici. Dr. Medici is one of a team of UC Davis doctors that oversee my care, with regard to my Wilson's disease. Dr. Medici is a gastroenterologist and liver specialist from Italy. She is young, vibrant, and in my opinion, brilliant! Additionally, she has great bedside manner and is very thorough. And, as you will see in a later chapter, Dr. Medici is truly a godsend!

It was a brisk, sunny morning as I headed to the doctor's office. The appointment went well. I am followed up by many specialists and have my liver enzymes and other blood work monitored at varying frequencies throughout the year. It was the middle of November, 2009, and I was feeling splendid, upbeat, and very blessed. I had my routine blood work completed that morning at the UC Davis lab after a physical examination by Dr. Medici who has once again given me a good report.

I was enjoying the mood I was in this morning, but am always left wondering how long it will last or what may trigger it to change. You see, one of the puzzling affects of Wilson's disease is that in a split-second, my mood can swing from great to awful or vice versa. For example, in November, my wife and I were on the balcony of a resort in Mexico, enjoying a breathtaking view of the Sea of Cortez in San Jose Del Cabo. I was singing, laughing, and having a blast, when I suddenly had the urge to jump off our 5th floor balcony and end it all. By this time I had not pondered suicide for more than a year, but many times in the past, while driving down the freeway, I would find myself debating whether or not I should just turn my truck into the median and end my life. Although I do not make plans or dwell on those thoughts, one can recognize just how disturbing those thoughts can be.

# Chapter 2
## Growing up

I had what I would consider a normal childhood. As stated in the introduction, other than being accident prone, I was a very healthy boy. I have two sisters, Cathy, who is a year older than me, and Jo Anne, who is seven years older than me. Any guy that has older sisters can empathize; my sisters tormented me, teased me, and made me cry, but they also loved me unconditionally.

I shared a bedroom with my sisters in our small, 800 square ft. home, seven miles north of Clarksdale, Mississippi. Imagine the privacy issues we had! My sisters would often tease me and say, "Mark's peering out the window" or "Mark slumbered in his bed," and I would get all upset and worked up, and eventually start crying.

I wet the bed until I was about 12 years old; my mom and dad would welcome me into their bed each time that happened. I slept on a single bed with a plastic mattress cover, the kind that crinkles when you move.

Hunting and fishing were both a part of growing up in the Mississippi Delta. I learned to shoot when I was about five, hunting along the wooded ditch that bordered the back side of our 4 ½ acres. I bagged my share of rabbits, doves, and frogs. Once, I shot a possum, another time, a raccoon. Both were good eating!

We fished during the summer months at Yazoo Pass. Daddy and I would dig gigantic night crawlers, put them in a coffee can, load up our cane fishing poles and the five of us would pile into the car and head up Highway 61. Sometimes we would catch a 2 or 3 pound catfish, but mostly, we caught small bluegills.

Every year my mother and father took us on a vacation. My dad liked to get where we were going as soon as possible and would drive up to 500 miles per day. Mama didn't drive, but she often argued with my dad over directions. I was always stuck in the back seat between my two sisters and I never got to sit by the window. Never!

\* \* \*

Being a teenager was no easy feat! I was not an atypical guy. My testosterone levels ran high and I was driven to find love or lust or whatever guys are looking for, and found myself straying from what the Lord would have me do.

I couldn't say if I broke the heart of more girls than girls broke mine... truthfully, I think it was pretty even. From the crush on Miss Bounds, a teacher at Coahoma County High School, to the serious relationship I had with Cynthia Roach, a girl that went to church with me, the number of "girlfriends" surpassed the number of fingers and toes I had.

I played football in high school and while playing Junior varsity I injured my left knee severely. The doctor injected my knee with cortisone which relieved the swelling, but left the pain to persist. After consultations with orthopedic surgeons at Memphis Baptist Hospital, I underwent a major surgery to remove my lateral meniscus which had been torn during a football game. My days of football were over.

The next time I walked onto the football field, I was escorting one of the Homecoming princesses or "maids" as they were called back then. The princess was Kathy Morris, a girl I drooled over every day but never had the courage to ask out. She was from an affluent family. The other Homecoming "maid" was Darrah Heaton, a girl that I sat next to in as many classes as I could. She too was from an affluent family... a rich plantation family! Surrounded by these beautiful ladies of the Homecoming "Court," I was in heaven that night!

\* \* \*

Did I mention that there were two classes of people in the deep South when I was growing up? I think it remains pretty much the same these days. No, it's not the blacks and the whites! It is the rich and the poor. My family was part of the poor class... the one that was made of both blacks and whites. It was the only class that blacks fit into back then, but if you were white and born into the rich class... you pretty much had it made, or so everyone thought.

Growing up poor gave me a great appreciation for life, work and education. Let me clarify one more thing about poor whites. There are poor whites, which we were (didn't have much money) but have a lot of love and spirit and family. Then there are the poor "white trash"... the kind you see on the Jerry Springer Show, where the mama falls in love with her daughter's boyfriend, and they say things like, "well it ain't gotta matta nohow cuz my huzban wuzn't sleepin wid me noways an my baby girl shudin beez hasin sexx noways!" These are the same people that frequent the local honky tonks and get all "liquored up" on paydays. My point is, that poor "white trash" is a subclass of the poor folks in the South.

\* \* \*

If girls and sports were not enough to keep the testosterone levels high, we had drag racing! My interest in cars was at an all time high by the time I got my drivers permit at age 14. My sister Jo Anne had eloped with Marlin Earl Anderson when I was 11. Marlin was nicknamed "Dinky" because of his small stature. Dinky was really into muscle cars and so was my sister. Dinky bought my sister a 1965 Mustang Fastback; this beauty was fire engine red and it was fast! That year we had a particularly hard freeze and the runways at Fletcher Field, a small private airport used primarily for crop dusters, had a thin layer of black ice. Planes were grounded due to weather conditions and school was out as well, so Dinky decided to take me for a thrilling adventure. Fletcher field was about one mile north of our house and my sister and Dinky lived in a house halfway between the airport and our home.

He picked me up around ten o'clock in the morning and drove me up to the airport where he stopped at the end of the runway. I knew what was about to take place. We fastened our seatbelts and he eased his foot down on the accelerator so the tire would get some traction on the ice. Gradually we picked up speed down the runway which was about a third of a mile long, roughly the length of six football fields laid end to end. When we reached a speed of between 80 and 90 miles per hour, Dinky turned the steering wheel all the way left sending us careening down the rest of the runway spinning like a top, one 360 after another! My heart was racing, but as soon as we came to rest near the edge of the runway, I shouted, "Let's do it again!"

As we headed back in the opposite direction, the speedometer of the red fastback swiftly approaching 80mph, I felt the rear of the car begin to fishtail, and in another split second, Dinky turned a hard right, causing the car to begin spinning in circles, spinning wrecklessly out of control. We spun out until the car reached the end of the runway where it slid to a halt on the frozen muddy field that lay alongside the pavement. Dinky pulled the car back onto the runway and drove to the south end. He turned the red beast around, revved the engine, looked over at me and asked, "Wanna try it?"

My mind was racing, I had a rush of adrenaline in my veins. I said "Heck yeah!" as I jumped out of the car to switch sides. The wind stung my face and hands. I sunk down into the driver's seat barely able to see above the steering wheel. I moved the seat closer so I could reach the pedals. As I fastened my seat belt, I listened attentively to Dinky's careful instructions. "Hold your foot on the brake and put it in drive," he said. It was an automatic with the shifter on the console. I struggled with the shifter until he said, "Squeeze the button underneath." I should have known this from watching both Dinky and Jo Anne drive me around town in their "hot rod muscle car."

I squeezed the T- shaped handle and pulled it down into "drive." I moved my right foot from the brake to the accelerator and pushed down. The wheels immediately began to spin and the car shuddered, "dancing" around on the ice. I panicked! Dinky, who was always up for a good thrill just looked over at me and casually said, "Ease up." I took my foot off the accelerator and the mustang which had hardly gained any speed, rolled to a stop. "Just ease down on the gas," Dinky said, "and when we get rolling, increase the pressure on the accelerator, and I'll tell you when to turn the wheel."

I was a little nervous and could feel my face flushed from the adrenaline. I leaned forward and at the same time stretched my right leg fully to reach the accelerator. My blue jeans made a squeaking sound as they rubbed against the red vinyl seat. I pushed ever so gently against the accelerator and the car crept forward like a snail. I wasn't going to blow it this time! I pushed down a little harder and we began rolling faster and faster. Glancing quickly down at the speedometer I was at 40 mph, five seconds later, I was at 50, then 60. Dinky said, "Turn it hard right." I think I closed my eyes as I turned the steering wheel to the right going hand over hand. I remember how easy the wheel turned as my small eleven year old hands grasped it. A few moments later the car came to a rest on its own. I opened my eyes. I was still alive and still in the driver's seat. Dinky looked at me, "Go again?" I didn't need any more encouragement... "Yep!" I said, and off I drove to the end of the runway to turn around.

Dinky and I spent a couple of hours spinning that Mustang at each end of the runway over and over and over. To this day, I never told my mom, and my dad went to his grave not knowing. But I made it home alive that day, mainly because God was with me!

* * *

I did have some very memorable moments growing up, none of which I could say contributed to my sometimes psychotic behavior... Many of the memorable moments involved guns, like the night I woke up at about 2 am and ran into the kitchen where several gunshots had sounded. There stood my dad in his boxers and muscleman t-shirt with a Colt .45 Army automatic pistol in his hand. The lights were on and I watched with awe as my dad placed another slug through a rat, about 14 inches long from its nose to the tip of its tail, as it climbed the lemon yellow window frame above the kitchen sink. The rat dropped into the sink beside another rat that had been victim of the shots that had awakened me.

Another incident I remember so vividly was on a trip to Washington, D.C. at Christmas time. Daddy had gotten us lost and we were somewhere in a "not so safe" part of the city, seemingly stuck going round and round in circles. Daddy usually splashed mud on the back of the car to cover up our Mississippi license plates whenever we went to "Yankee country," but apparently the rain and snow that we had traveled through in our 2,000 mile journey had washed away the mud revealing our origin.    A cabdriver pulled alongside us and shouted at my father to "go back where you came from!"    As I sat in between my two sisters in the back seat of our 1965 black Oldsmobile F-85 with red vinyl interior, daddy reached under his seat and then turning to me he handed me that same Colt .45 Army Automatic and said, "Mark, if that guy gets near us again, lean out the window and put a bullet through his radiator!"  Daddy reached under this seat again, this time to retrieve a Smith & Wesson .32 caliber "Lady Smith" with pearl handles.  He handed the pistol to my oldest sister repeating the instructions he had given me.

No incident from my childhood or my past, I can safely say, led to my varying psychological and emotional states.  Dr. Spock may disagree, but from my perspective, nothing in my childhood can be linked to depression, thoughts of suicide, or irrational thinking.

# Chapter 3
## From South to North then East to West

My dad sold his business in the Fall of 1970 and was hired as an engineering technician for the U.S. Department of Agriculture in Beltsville, Maryland. My mother worked for the Sears Catalogue Center in Clarksdale. Cathy was a high school senior with plans to attend Mississippi State University and I was a junior at Coahoma County High School. We moved to Tacoma Park, Maryland in the summer of '71 and I was enrolled in Northwestern High School, close to the University of Maryland, College Park campus. I graduated in the top 20 percent of the class of '72 which had over 650 graduates. My sister had graduated from Coahoma County High School the year before, salutatorian, second in her class of 54 graduates.

* * *

I went straight to the University of Maryland, College Park after graduating from Northwestern High School in Hyattsville, Maryland. I enrolled in zoology and algebra, two subjects that I loved. Success in high school had been no problem and I felt I was completely prepared for college. Something, however, was changing in my abilities, my mental aptitude, and most importantly, my attitude. I was no longer the fun-loving, nice young man that had graduated from Northwestern High School. I was unable to focus, became very moody, got into minor skirmishes with people at work, and often snapped at my parents.

Unbeknownst to me, Wilson's disease was taking its toll on my health. The inability to focus, irrational behavior, and anger and depression were all signs that would suggest some underlying disease.

My interest in girls had not waned, however, and whenever I had an opportunity to get close to a young woman, or an older woman for that matter, I jumped at the chance. I was invited by a female from my zoology class to go to a Mensa party. I didn't know what Mensa was and she said it was a society of very bright people and she felt I would fit in. We went together and the facilitator invited me to take the appropriate tests to see if I qualified to be a member of Mensa. I signed up for the California mental maturity test as well as the Catell I.Q. test. Much to my surprise, I scored in the top 1% with an IQ of 145. I joined Mensa and attended a couple of parties in Georgetown. Regardless of my scholastic abilities, I felt so out of place that I ultimately moved on to other things.

\* \* \*

I worked a few different jobs from building maintenance for an apartment complex to various construction jobs until I joined the Navy in 1974. I boarded a plane in Baltimore, Maryland which was to transport the group of six recruits, including myself, to boot camp in Orlando, Florida. It was late in March and the air was hot and humid when we disembarked in Orlando. The war in Viet Nam was winding down and the boys were coming home, but I still hoped to see some action. I had scored high marks on the exam for aptitude and went in as an E-3, rank of Seaman. I had signed on for six years and was going to be an Electronics Technician, but after six months, I began having severe issues with my left knee, the one I had injured playing football. After all of this, the Navy decided it was best to ship me back home.

\* \* \*

Following my brief enlistment in the Navy, I moved back home for a while and then transplanted to Arlington, Virginia to share an apartment with Dinky. He and JoAnne had divorced, and he had girls over at the apartment all the time. I eventually hooked up with one of Dinky's girlfriends. She worked for the CIA and was a flaming redhead. Trish was two years older than me which made her even more appealing than her red hair. After we dated for a couple of months, she decided to move back home to Albuquerque, New Mexico, and I, like a little puppy dog, followed her. After struggling on my own in Albuquerque for five months, working as a janitor at K-Mart, and struggling to maintain a relationship with a girlfriend that no longer had time for me, I returned home to Maryland with my tail between my legs.

\* \* \*

The next move I made was three years later when I moved from the east coast to the west, to sunny, southern California. My sister, Cathy, lived in Canoga Park with her husband David and they let me live with them until I could establish myself. I went to work for Big 5 Sporting Goods and was soon promoted to Assistant Manager and moved from Canoga Park to the store in Burbank where I met a lot of actors. Before I could move out of my sister's townhouse, though, I had a motorcycle accident in which I broke my left leg - the femur - right at the joint that had been injured in high school football.

After a complete recovery, I was transferred to the Van Nuys store, where I met Suzanne and Dana, who were both cashiers. Suzanne was a couple of years older than me, Italian and very ladylike. Dana, on the other hand, was tomboyish, rode horses, usually had her hair in a long braid and liked going out late at night. Did I mention, Suzanne liked to turn in early? Anyhow, I began dating both of them, something neither was aware of initially. Some nights I would take Suzanne home early, and call Dana to come over. All was well until they started comparing notes!

# Chapter 4
## Wild, Wild West

Dating employees is never recommended, especially when you are in a management position. A year after beginning with Big 5, I lost my job for fraternizing with cashiers.

There were a couple of positions open at Newhall Land and Farming Company about 30 miles North of the San Fernando Valley where I lived, and I landed a job with them. In addition to a salary, I was put up in a two bedroom ranch house with stables where the horses that were used for cattle driving were kept. The house sat right off the bank of the Piru River in the middle of orange and grapefruit groves and my responsibilities included caring for the horses and helping round up stray cattle. The terrain up from the groves was rather rocky with loose shale everywhere. I was starting my second season with the company when a fellow horseman named Bill and I dismounted our horses to get a calf that was stuck in some heavy brush. No sooner had I dismounted that I lost my footing and went sliding down this steep mountainside. I grasped at rocks and branches and saplings. Finally, after tumbling for about 75 feet, I planted my bad leg into the unstable ground and stopped. I had been accident prone as a child; now I was 24 and sometimes seemed uncoordinated and had difficulty with balance. Despite my numerous visits to doctors and hospitals, no doctors saw this pattern of neurological signs that may suggest Wilson's disease.

\* \* \*

I spent the next week in Northridge Hospital after a major surgery that repaired ripped ligaments and a torn medial meniscus. It was at Northridge Hospital where I found myself crossing lines I never imagined. One of the nurses that cared for me was Fran, another Italian woman, this one from New York with an accent that completely gave it away!

I am not sure what exactly attracted me to Fran, or Fran to me for that matter, but the attraction was there and it was strong. Fran was at my bedside for most of the week that I was in the hospital. Not only did she nurse me back to health, she messed around with me. There was this big problem, though; Fran was married, and she had a child at home, but that didn't stop us. When I got out of the hospital, we continued to see each other. Her husband worked out of town a lot, and when she knew he would be gone for a couple of days, she would have me come over and stay with her, but that's not all…

Fran smoked pot often, and I had tried some before. We started getting high together and then, because she was a nurse, she had access to "'Ludes, Reds, and Tooies," all sedative-hypnotic drugs or "downers" as well as Black Beauties and Yellow Jackets, known as "uppers" or speed pills. When she was off work, we would party for hours and hours. This was just the beginning of my journey down a long and wrong path.

* * *

I had been reassigned by Newhall Land and Farming Company to running a hardware store that the company owned in Valencia. The salary I made was less than before. The upside was that I was still able to stay in the ranch house. The downside, however, was that it was a 45 minute drive from the San Fernando Valley where Fran lived. It was boring work; there would often be no more than a dozen customers in a day. I began looking for work in the San Fernando Valley and Fran called me one day to tell me that a friend informed her of a manager position in Canoga Park at a local bar called "Mr. Casper's."

I jumped in the car and headed down to the valley and arrived at the same time as the lunch crowd. Mr. Casper's was not just a bar, it was a topless go-go bar! I found the barmaid and inquired about the position. The barmaid, Kitty, sported cutoff shorts with most of her business hanging out the back and a skimpy halter top that was tied in the front. When she leaned over the bar, everything in front was exposed!

Kitty pointed me to the office door where she said I would find Arnie, the owner. The door opened when I knocked and I took two steps up into the cramped office that couldn't have been more than 8 feet by 10 feet. There was a brown, vinyl couch on one side and a black love seat on the other with a desk at the far end of the love seat. The room was filled with smoke; two half-clad dancers sat on the couch, one drinking a beer, the other a glass of wine. Arnie had a lit cigarette dangling from his lips as he counted money in a register drawer. He stopped, picked up his glass of wine from the desk and took a sip. He asked me if I was looking for a job and if I was reliable. I said yes to both questions and then he said, "You're hired. Can you start tonight?" I nodded my head.

The night crowd was much different from the daytime lunch crowd. I was getting to know all the dancers and barmaids as they jockeyed themselves into positions for favoritism when I heard what sounded like thunder out back. A minute or two later a half dozen Hell's Angels strolled in through the back door. Was I in over my head? Only time would tell.

I worked almost every night at Mr. Casper's and on the nights that I didn't work, I partied. Fran and I had moved on, but there were plenty of other proverbial fish in the sea. The dancers were always coming and going and Arnie had moved me to the position of hiring and firing. It was like I was a part of a song that played every day in Mr. Casper's...

Eric Burdon and War's "Spill the Wine"

> *There I was. I was taken to a place, the Hall of the Mountain King. I stood high upon a mountaintop, naked with the world in front of every kind of girl. There were strong ones, tall ones, short ones, brown ones, black ones, round ones, big ones, crazy ones. Out of the middle came a lady. She whispered in my ear, something crazy. She said:*

*Spill the wine, dig that girl.* [1]
*Spill the wine.*
*Spill the wine, dig that girl.*
*Dig that girl.*

*I could feel the hot flame of fire roaring in my back as she disappeared. But soon, she returned. In her hand was a bottle of wine; in the other, a glass. She poured some of the wine from the bottle into the glass, and raised it to her lips, and just before she drank, she said:*

*Take the wine, take that girl.*
*Spill the wine, dig that girl.*

\* \* \*

Keeping the peace in a place where scantily clad women, mingling among bikers and businessmen alike, with free-flowing drugs and booze mixed in, was no easy task. Mr. Casper's was frequented by bikers, but was well known as Hells Angels'

---

[1] Note: Ironically, the lyrics that I heard (the same as written above) are misunderstood, much like I have been many times in my life. The correct lyrics to the song are "Spill the wine, take that pearl."

territory or just "Angels'," territory as they were referred to, and many of the dancers were the "old ladies" or "property" of individual "Angels." I maintained an allegiance with the Hells Angels. I protected their "old ladies" from perverts when they were gone, and they "had my back" whenever trouble broke out in the bar. I had begun partying after hours with Dennis, aka "Red," and "Tiny", the president of the Hells Angels' San Fernando Valley chapter. Dennis and I had become pretty good friends. He was nicknamed "Red" because he had bright red hair and a bright red beard. His girlfriend, Suzanne (different from the Suzanne I had dated), was one of my most reliable dancers (reliable in the sense that she loved to work and would fill any shift if someone called in sick). Suzanne had a slight build and was in her early twenties. She had pock marks all over her arms, legs, and face, caused by the picking and scratching at her skin while "cranked up" or "speeding" on Crystal Methamphetamine, or "Crank" as it is known on the street.

\* \* \*

One night, I threw a big party at a little 3-bedroom house that I had rented in Van Nuys.

Dennis and Suzanne, Cathy (a barmaid and very close friend of mine) and her boyfriend, Barney (a wannabe Hells Angel), were there, along with dozens of bikers and their old ladies. There was every kind of drug imaginable flowing freely. The party broke up about 6:00 a.m. I caught a few winks on my couch, while Suzanne crashed in my bed. Dennis, a carpenter by day, headed off to work. He was a productive member of society, but was feared by many when he was mixing booze and drugs.

That evening Dennis returned to the house with his tools and a couple boxes of clothes. He told me that he and Suzanne were moving in with me. How do you say no to a Hells Angel?

# Chapter 5
Delivered Again and Yet Again

The Hells Angels weren't the worst of my troubles. I was into using drugs fairly heavily and within three months of "Red" and Suzanne moving in, we were all moving out of the cute little house, having been evicted by the landlord. I found a studio apartment that I moved into by myself and continued working at Mr. Casper's, and, because I was well liked by everyone, John, the owner of another topless bar "Batman A-Go-Go," wanted me to come to work for him and I couldn't pass up the offer. Not only was he Arnie's competitor, although I really felt no loyalty to Arnie, John also offered me a better deal.

That's when my life went from bad to worse. Cathy, the barmaid mentioned earlier, worked for John. One night after I had gotten off work, Cathy called me and said she needed to come over, that she needed a place to stay. When she arrived, she had not one, but two black eyes… Barney, her boyfriend, had beat her severely. She said she needed a place to stay for a couple of days, which turned into weeks. Cathy had a daughter, Danielle, who was about eight years old at the time. Danielle stayed with Cathy's mother, a real estate agent that lived in Encino. I took Cathy to visit her mom and daughter. I remember sitting around the pool that evening drinking wine with Cathy, her mom, and a friend of Cathy's from high school, Lorraine.

I felt I wanted to be more than just a friend to Cathy. She was beautiful and seemed bright, but Barney, her boyfriend, had really messed her up, both physically and emotionally. Cathy was always strung out or high. Come to think of it, I remember very few moments spent with her when she was sober.

One night, she called me at the bar and asked me to pick up some downers from a dealer we knew that worked at the post office. The postman frequented the Batman A-Go-Go at lunch and every evening and we went in my office where the postman handed me a jar of 200 "tooies". "Tooie" is the street name for a drug known as amobarbital, a powerful sedative or "downer." I took the jar to my '65 Mustang that was parked out back, put the jar in the trunk and lodged it in behind the spare tire so that it wouldn't roll around, then headed to the apartment.

It was a little after midnight. Rain was coming down hard and the wind was blowing the rain in sheets. I left the bar at Sherman Way and Reseda Boulevard heading east on Sherman Way. I lived on Vanowen Street just past Louise Avenue. I turned south on Lindley Avenue because traffic was usually lighter (Traffic is heavy 24 hours a day in Southern California), and as I approached Vanowen, I could barely see the green left arrow on the traffic light. I turned left just as a kid rode his bicycle out into the intersection. Wham! The boy lay sprawled out on the hood of the car, rain pelting his thrashing body.

I kept my cool. This was 1980, long before cell phones. There were a lot of people gathering around. The police and paramedics were there within minutes and the paramedics strapped the boy, who was writhing and screaming with pain, onto a backboard and loaded him into the ambulance. One police began questioning me as to what had happened, while other officers gathered witnesses' statements. My heart was racing and all I could think about was the jar of 200 "tooies" in the trunk. What if they asked me to open the trunk? Did I look suspicious? I made a deal with God right on the spot... yeah, God, the One that I had distanced myself from over the past few years. I said God, deliver me from this mess and I will turn my life back to You. Did I mean it? I wanted to. But something had gotten a hold of me, and it was hard turning back to Him. I think it was a combination of the joys of the world and my own pride that had separated me from God.

Matthew 6:24 says,

*"No man can serve two masters: for either he will hate the one, and love the other; or else he will hold to the one, and despise the other."*

I had fallen prey to Satan's world of selfishness. I didn't have any room for God, but when I was in a jam, I was quick to try and strike a deal with Him.

The police let me go home that night. I had made a legal turn and the boy had ridden his bike into the crosswalk on a "don't walk" sign. The police said I could not have avoided the accident. They tried to contact the kid's mother and father. Turns out they had left the 12 year-old at home alone and were out partying. The boy had a broken leg and a messed up bicycle, and I still had my freedom, or so I thought!

\* \* \*

The next jam I was in, in retrospect, was scarier than the car accident. There was this girl that waitressed part-time at a bar that I frequented on my nights off. Tami was her name, and I remember having a strong desire to get to know her better.

One night, I was at an "after hours" party at one of the local drug dealer's house. The dealer's name was Lance. Lance had a long wavy ponytail and he did drugs only on occasion. They say the secret to making a profit dealing drugs is not to use drugs yourself, and that was Lance's motto. One thing about "after hours" parties is that as the word of a party spreads, the party grows to 20, 30, 40 sometimes more than 100 partygoers.

Well, I had been there for about a half an hour when I spotted Tami, and she motioned me over. She said, "Why don't you come into the bathroom with me?" as she reached for my hand with hers. I did not require any persuasion at that point, but the event that followed certainly could have sealed my fate.

In the bathroom, Tami, so beautiful with her medium length brown hair, sat down on the toilet. She had on hot pants and a tube top... both stylish in 1981. She looked at me and said, "I want you to shoot up with me." I looked at her and said "What?" I guess I was subconsciously stalling, searching for a way out of the situation. She said, "Come on. Come on. Please, please, please... shoot up with me. I have this really pure coke!" At that moment everything seemed so surreal.

Now, I had taken an oath with myself to never stick a needle in my arm. I had witnessed dancers shoot everything from Cocaine to Delada to Heroine. I remembered one dancer named LaDonna, a beautiful girl with long dark hair, who would nod off on stage while she was dancing. Once, I found her in the dressing room shooting heroine under her toenails so there would be no "tracks" or marks left from shooting up.

Now, I was in the bathroom at a party with Tami, and I was about to come face to face with the true me. Tami pulled a "kit" out of her purse, containing a latex tube, a small spoon, and a syringe all wrapped in a small scarf. She took a vial and a cigarette lighter from her hip pocket. Being with my dream girl had suddenly become a nightmare, and my only hope was that this was a bad dream and I would soon wake up! After putting a few of drops of water into the spoon, she dumped some cocaine into the spoon. She handed me the lighter and told me to hold it lit under the spoon. The coke dissolved and she quickly drew it up in the syringe.

She handed me the latex tube and said "Hurry... tie me off!" She made a fist as I tightened the rubber tube around her biceps, and as quickly as she had grabbed my hand that evening, she slid the thin gauged needle into a vein just below her elbow joint. A drop of blood appeared at the base of the syringe and then she pushed it forward.

"What should I do?" I kept asking myself. I wanted her very badly and there I was in the bathroom with her. She looked up at me and smiled. "Your turn." I felt as if I had no choice. What if I do this? What comes next? What will my mom and dad think if they ever find out? All these questions raced through my head, but not once did I cry out to God. In that moment, I did not even give Him a thought. Yet He was there!

Yes, God was there, and right in front of Him, I chose to do the wrong thing, the selfish thing, the most damaging thing I could do to myself right at that moment. I said, "Let's do it!" Tami was beginning to really space out, but together we prepared a "fix" for me. I did not have the steady hand to put a needle in my vein, so Tami did it for me.

Now you are probably wondering why I would say God was there with me as I made the wrong choice... the choice to continue living my life despicably. This is what I believe and this is what I want you to know. While Tami got "higher than a kite" as the proverbial saying goes, I did not even get a small buzz out of that cocaine directly in the vein. I was a child of God. Once I became a child of God, He never disowned me. He allowed me to choose my own path and, though the path I had chosen was wrong, so very wrong, I recognized that it was by His grace I was delivered from the slavery that could have resulted had I gotten a "high" out of that shot.

* * *

A few weeks after that incident, Arnie called me back to work at Mr. Casper's and opened his home to me. He had a nice house where he lived with his wife, Cyndi. Arnie was in his late 50's and Cyndi was twenty-something. She was always vibrant, a ray of sunshine, but she drank heavily. One night, I got a call at the bar from one of Arnie's old buddies. He said to find someone to watch the bar and get home fast. I put one of the dancer's boyfriends in charge and took off.

As I arrived at the house, there were police cars up and down both sides of the quiet suburban street. Someone had called Arnie's daughter Lori who met me on the sidewalk. I remember so vividly how

Lori fell into my arms, mascara running all down her cheeks. She could hardly speak… "Cyndi's dead," she said. "She shot herself."

\* \* \*

Cyndi was high on drugs and alcohol. She had taken Arnie's .38 special, put it up to her temple and pulled the trigger. Cyndi had expressed her belief in God and we had even talked about Christ's suffering. I cannot say for sure where Cyndi's soul is now, I did not know her heart. What I do know is Cyndi's death was a major turning point in my life!

After Cyndi's funeral, I had to find my direction again. I stayed with different people, but trying to sever those old ties proved to be more difficult than I imagined. Soon, I found myself out on the street, living in my car with only a few possessions and the clothes on my back. I called my parents and they arranged for a bus ticket to get up to the San Francisco Bay area where my sister Cathy had moved. A week later, they bought a plane ticket for me to fly back to Maryland. I had nowhere else to go. The prodigal son was returning home, humiliated. The year was 1981, and I was about to celebrate my 27th birthday.

# Chapter 6
## First Manifestations

From 1973 until 1982, my behavior varied from sweet and innocent to mean and worldly. I did not maintain any dedicated relationships with friends or family except for my sister Cathy, my mother and father. These changes in my personality were hardly noticeable and only became a problem when I moved from my transient existence in Southern California back home to Laurel, Maryland in 1981, when my parents initially noticed severe mood swings. In February of 1982, I had obtained a position at Laurel racetrack hot walking horses. I had always had a great interest in horses, and being able to work with thoroughbred race horses gave me great satisfaction. I was quickly promoted to the position of groom. I took great pride in my work and gained significant knowledge about training and caring for racehorses.

Life on the racetrack was far from easy. My day began at four o'clock in the morning with feeding the livestock, followed by grooming and preparing the three or four horses in my care for exercise riders that arrived around 6 A.M. Preparing them included wrapping the horses' legs with bandages for support, picking and painting their hooves and tacking them up. As the horse was taken out for exercise, I would clean its stall and change the water. When the exercise rider returned from the track, I would untack the horse and have a hot walker take the horse for a walk to cool it down.

There were times when I was needed to walk the horses, and as I would walk a horse around the shed row, I noticed my right hand would begin to tremble, causing the chain of the lead (attached to the horse's halter) to jingle. A lead is a long leather or nylon strap with a chain and snap that you hook into the horse's halter to "lead" it. The trembling of my hand rapidly worsened and I became known around the race track as "Shakey." My coworkers often teased me, accusing me of having withdrawals, but within one month of the onset of this tremor, my walk became crippled. I dragged my right leg and my whole body was leaned to the right including my head which was cocked even further over than my body. I was scared of what was happening and my parents became increasingly concerned.

I continued to work at the racetrack moving from trainer to trainer. One trainer was very sympathetic as was a female groom. Bill and Barbara were like angels, unbeknownst to me at the time. As my health steadily deteriorated, my parents contacted a cousin who was a medical doctor in Virginia. He made a special appointment for me, and I went to his Virginia office for an evaluation and consultation. My cousin, Ray, was a dermatologist, but because he was a medical doctor and showed interest and concern for me, we decided this would be a good start. Ray personally took my vitals, which were normal, and he drew blood for a lab workup. Ray also determined that I had a mild form of "palsy" and sent me off with a prescription which he thought may control the tremors.

After taking the medication for more than two weeks, my condition had worsened dramatically and I was having uncontrolled "wing flapping" episodes followed by outbursts of anger and tears! At 27 years of age, I now needed assistance to button my pants and tie my shoes. I thanked God between episodes of bitterness for my loving mother and father. I could tell that worry over my condition was taking a toll on my father who was struggling with his own health concerns and I cried out to the Lord in anger and self-pity, asking him to relieve me of this trying disease, even if it meant taking me home. I was constantly reminded of David's cry to God to listen to Him in Psalm 39:12.

*"Hear my prayer, O LORD, and give ear unto my cry; hold not thy peace at my tears: for I am a stranger with thee, and a sojourner, as all my fathers were."*

I remembered Paul's situation of the thorn in his side that he asked God to remove three times to no avail. I was not comforted by these scriptures! I didn't realize, at the time, that God had great plans for me... and some difficult lessons to learn. God knew that I was not trusting Him fully, that I had relied on my own abilities to see me through life up to this point. He knew that this disease would rob me of many of my abilities, but only temporarily, until I fell back into His arms.

That day had not come yet. What I had to come to realize was, God had a purpose and a plan all laid out for me. I was not there yet!

# Chapter 7
## My Diagnosis

It had been almost a year since my cousin had prescribed medication for my "palsy" like symptoms. My tremors had progressed dramatically, and I had lost more than thirty pounds! My father had contacted our United States senator and representative regarding my problem. With their help, they petitioned National Institutes of Health (NIH) and were successful in having me evaluated by two neurologists.

I went with my mother and father to see Dr. Newman and Dr. Schultz, two clinicians conducting research on rare neurological diseases at NIH. I have to say that while having my parent's love and support at this evaluation was a blessing, there were parts of the questioning that were extremely uncomfortable! When asked about past drug use including amphetamines, barbiturates, cocaine, or marijuana, my mind began racing! How do I answer these questions? I began to think, I don't want my mother or father to know that I've been involved in drugs... but then I thought, what if this has a major bearing on what is happening in my life right now? If I'm not totally honest, could this affect my diagnosis? Or even worse, my prognosis?

Scriptures began to shoot through my head and I began to think about my heavenly father and how he feels when I do things that are not God honoring. You see I was totally ashamed of my past, never expecting to have to reveal these dark secrets right there in front of parents. My tremor began to worsen, my voice shook as I answered in the affirmative. My parents didn't even look at me and I felt so ashamed. Never did they bring the subject up. It was like God, when He says I will put your sins as far to the east as to the west.

Under Dr. Schultz and Dr. Newman's care, I underwent a battery of neurological tests. They analyzed my speech, tested my fine motor skills, had me walk heel to toe, touch my nose with my finger with my eyes closed, switch hands and repeat; they asked questions about my sex drive, my appetite, my mental state including how often I was depressed, anxious, angry, melancholy. After what seemed like several hours of tests, they arranged for me to see the ophthalmologist that same afternoon. The ophthalmologist gave me a thorough eye examination and said that in his slit-lamp exam he noticed that I had copper color rings around the irises of both eyes. The ophthalmologist recognized that, even though I appeared very concerned about what was happening, I was very interested in the findings and spoke with a high level of scientific knowledge. He explained to me that the rings around my irises were Kaiser-Fleischer rings, a pathognomonic sign of Wilson's disease which is a rare genetic disorder that affects the liver.

Little was said on the way home to my parents' townhome in Laurel, Maryland, but I sensed that the events of the day weighed very heavy on their hearts. As we ate dinner that night, silence ruled the room. I knew the doctors had spoken with my parents while I was with the ophthalmologist, but they weren't offering up any information and I sure wasn't asking!

* * *

It was about 9 P.M. when the phone rang. I was lying in bed in the room across the hall from my parent's room. My mother summoned me into the room and handed me the phone. I took a deep breath, then said, "Hello?" "Is this William Mark Dendy?" the voice on the other end asked. It was Dr. Newman. "Yes it is," I said. "Mr. Dendy... Dr. Schultz and I, after careful evaluation of your neurological test results and the report from the ophthalmologist, believe that you have a rare genetic condition known as Wilson's Disease, and we would like to know if you would be..." Tears began to streak down my cheeks - tears of sadness, tears of joy, tears of wonder. I was struggling to maintain my composure as my mother and father both had their eyes trained on my face, trying to ascertain from my reaction what the news was.

"Excuse me, Dr. Newman, could you please repeat what you just said?" I said with my quivering voice. "Yes, Mr. Dendy... we believe you have Wilson's Disease and would like you to be a part of our research study in the NIH Research Hospital." I had turned my back to my parents to hide my disconcerted look. I turned back around and, holding the phone to my chest, I said, "They think I have Wilson's disease and they want me to be a part of a research study at the hospital." "Tell them we'll call them tomorrow," my dad said. I raised the phone back to my ear and said, "My dad would like to know if we can call you tomorrow." "Take all the time you need," Dr. Newman said.

"We think we can help you, but take your time and call us when you're ready."

* * *

I struggled to get to sleep that night. I had been avoiding talking to God and now it seemed as though He had provided the doctors that might have the answers to some of my questions. At the same time, there was one question that Satan was pressing me to ask... why did God allow this to happen to me? You see, I have come to recognize that Satan raises all sorts of questions in one's mind to raise doubts about God's existence or our purpose in life. And the question that so many have asked before me, and so many will ask after I am dead and gone is, why would God allow this to happen to me?

I couldn't bring myself to ask that question to God, perhaps it was that little bit of selflessness that I had conjured up while waiting at the doctor's clinic earlier that day. I thought my condition was severe, but, while at the clinic, God had opened my eyes to a whole new population of individuals: men and women, boys and girls, whose conditions my condition paled by comparison. No, this wasn't a "new" population... these were the people that you and I are guilty of walking past everyday and ignoring as if they don't even exist. These are the "lepers" of today's society - the people you see that have epilepsy, multiple sclerosis, muscular dystrophy (the kids and adults Jerry Lewis has devoted much of his life to helping), Parkinson's disease, and a myriad of others. The droolers, the uncoordinated, the ones that struggle with speech, the ones that require diapers at age 15, 20, and so on because they do not have control of basic bodily functions. And here I was, at age 27, becoming one of them nearly overnight! I closed my eyes and steadied my right hand with my left. "God, please let all this come to an end," I prayed.

* * *

I got up early the next morning and went to the race track to work. I was preoccupied with the events of the previous day and as I stood in the shed row with a horse tacked up waiting for an exercise rider, there was another groom, a young man from Haiti, I believe, about 10 feet in front of me with a horse also tacked up. His exercise rider had arrived and was holding the horse's bridle while the young man picked the horse's hooves. In the blink of an eye, the horse pulled his left rear foot from the groom's strong hand, cocked and fired his left leg with such power, it lifted the groom off his feet and sent him flying. The guy landed at my feet semi-conscious. My horse startled, but thank God, I maintained control and quickly ushered it into the nearest stall. I ran back out to the young man whose forehead was bleeding, the result of the horse having squarely connected with its shod hoof. An ambulance was there moments later, and God had shown me just how dispensable each life is and how quickly circumstances could be changed. [2]

\* \* \*

That afternoon, I spoke with my mom and dad about going into the hospital. Although I was an adult and knew the decision was ultimately mine, I respected my parents and knew they were as concerned as I was about the condition of my health. I sought their guidance and wisdom and, despite the fact that this was something of magnitude that we were still struggling to comprehend, a decision had to be made and the

---

[2] Note: The young man suffered a concussion but was back to work within a couple of days.

longer we "sat on it," the more complex matters would get.

In retrospect, I see that God had essentially laid this in our laps and quietly whispered to me and my parents, "Trust me... I am here with you. You, my child, belong to Me, and I would see you through this!" How an unbeliever gets through tough times like this, I will never know, but for me it is comforting to know, WITHOUT A SHADOW OF DOUBT, that God is concerned about me and is present in my everyday life. All He asks of you and me is the same as He whispered to me back on that difficult and trying day - to trust Him and He will remain faithful and keep His promises.

* * *

My parents and I agreed that it was probably in my best interest to enroll into the research study on Wilson's disease. I called Dr. Newman and discussed the specifics including a required six weeks of hospitalization in order for them to collect enough data, run enough tests, and establish the best therapeutic protocols for my individual case. Additionally, because I was local, I could spend weekends at home since the research was conducted Monday through Friday. He emphasized the importance of the commitment to the study and stated that they would do everything within their power to help me and my family understand what the future would hold for me, as well as provide me with the best treatment for such a rare disease.

Because I was able to be home on weekends, I decided to work out a weekend arrangement with the horse trainer I worked for, Mr. Bill Dixon, who hesitantly agreed. Two girls that also worked for Mr. Dixon, a groom named Barbara and a hot walker named Marley, came over to find out what was going on. Barbara and Marley were genuinely concerned about me and came to visit me many times over the course of the next six weeks in the hospital at NIH.

Easter Sunday, 1957 - Mama said I was the prettiest boy.

My Dad in the army in 1942, stationed in California guarding the beaches of Southern California.

My mom in 1945 at her high school graduation in Washington, D.C., four months before meeting my dad at a USO dance in Ft. Belvoir, Virginia.

Me in my "quick-draw" pose, Christmas of 1960. Back then the Lone Ranger was my hero.

My sister, Cathy, me, my daddy, and sister, JoAnne in the spring of 1955.

JoAnne, Cathy, and me, Christmas of 1957. Check out our "Charlie Brown" Christmas tree.

Homecoming in eighth grade. I escorted Kathy
Morris. We looked regal!

My senior prom, 1972, with my girlfriend Cynthia Roach's best friend, Karen Brineman. Check out that tuxedo and those spats!

Getting ready to make my third jump from a Cessna 182 at Pelican Landing on the Eastern Shore of Maryland in 1975.

Six years later, I couldn't shave without cutting myself. I weighed in at just over 130 pounds, 60 pounds less than I weighed in high school.

The small house that I grew up in with my mom, dad, and two older sisters.

Daddy drives up our dirt (mud in winter) driveway in his new 1965 Oldsmobile F-85, black with red vinyl interior and no air conditioning, no power steering, and no power brakes.

My family in March 2010 - Me, my wife Zeta, my sons A.J. and Steven, and my daughter, the "apple of my eye," Lyndsie.

# Chapter 8
## Difficult to understand

Proponents of evolution discount God, often arguing that God is an invention of man. Many claim that if God is love then why would He allow disease, terrible situations, catastrophes such as Hurricane Katrina and the recent earthquake in Haiti and the like to occur among mankind. My colleagues have told me that my condition exists because of mutations that have occurred in the human genome. The plain and simple truth is that my genetic condition is a direct result of the fall of man as stated in the book of Genesis. Furthermore, I believe that God is the ultimate engineer of life as can be seen in the complexities of all living things.

As a professor of biology, I am often confronted with my view on evolution. I believe that evolution is seen daily in our living world; however, the evolution I'm speaking of is microevolution and a prime example is demonstrated through antibiotic resistance acquired in bacteria. Whenever a doctor prescribes antibiotics they give strict instruction to take the whole regimen even if you get better before you're completely out of the prescribed medicine. The explanation for this is quite simple. If you stop the antibiotics before the prescribed course is complete, any surviving bacteria will most likely have developed resistance to the specific antibiotic used. Many scientific studies have been conducted that support this type of evolution. This has much to do with bacteria's exponential rate of reproduction.

On the other hand, there is no empirical evidence that macroevolution, the evolution of new species through changes in existing species over thousands of years, actually takes place. The argument that evolutionists use is that the many mutations that occur in order for a new species to evolve must be beneficial, however, most mutations that occur in any given species' genome are harmful rather than beneficial.

\* \* \*

Wilson's disease, also known as hepatolenticular degeneration, was described in 1912 by Samuel

Alexander Kinnear Wilson, a British neurologist. In his 211 page doctoral thesis, "Progressive Lenticular Degeneration: A familial nervous disease associated with cirrhosis of the liver," Wilson detailed the lenticular and hepatic aspects of the disease which had been previously described and known as Westphal-Strümpell's pseudosclerosis. At the time, Wilson was 33 years of age and received the prestigious gold medal of the University of Edinburgh. The following year, Wilson published a paper in the academic journal *Brain*, in which he discussed his observations of four affected patients. In his paper, Wilson focused attention upon the important role of the basal ganglia within this disorder. This paper earned him great recognition and his name became connected with the disease, labeling the condition known as hepatolenticular degeneration, Wilson's disease. Later, Wilson insisted that the familial disease be called Kinnear Wilson's disease. One conclusion Wilson drew in his published paper was the nervous disorder was not congenital or inherited; his conclusion was that it was sometimes familial.

* * *

The question that is often posed by others and

sometimes by myself is "Why me?" Why am I the one that is burdened with this disease that affects me in a myriad of ways. As I grow older and wiser, I have come to realize that God has a special purpose in allowing me to suffer from this disease. Jeremiah 1:5 makes it evident to me that this is all a part of God's plan to strengthen me:

*Before I formed thee in the belly I knew thee; and before thou camest forth out of the womb I sanctified thee, and I ordained thee a prophet unto the nations.*

and the first verses of Psalm 139 echo the fact that God is very aware of my Wilson's disease:

*1 O lord, thou hast searched me, and known me.*
*2 Thou knowest my downsitting and mine uprising, thou understandest my thought afar off.*
*3 Thou compassest my path and my lying down, and art acquainted with all my ways.*
*4 For there is not a word in my tongue, but, lo, O LORD, thou knowest it altogether.*
*5 Thou hast beset me behind and before, and laid thine hand upon me.*
*6 Such knowledge is too wonderful for me; it is high, I cannot attain unto it.*

At the time I was diagnosed, Wilson's disease was

an obscure hereditary disease where excess copper was not properly metabolized, but thanks to medical doctors like Dr. Valentina Medici, my personal physician, and Dr. George Brewer, who have dedicated their research efforts to understanding this rare condition, Wilson's disease is better understood and there are safer and more effective treatments.

One minor point I wish to clarify is that the disease is now known as Wilson disease. I refer to my condition as Wilson's disease simply because that is what I was diagnosed with and that is what has stuck with me. Since I was diagnosed, nearly three decades ago, the knowledge of Wilson's disease has vastly expanded.

Wilson disease, a genetic disorder that prevents the body from eliminating excess copper, has the potential to be life threatening since the human body requires only a small amount of copper. Copper, a ubiquitous metal, is present in many foods and is even found in water that passes through copper pipes. It is now known that Wilson's disease is caused by the inheritance of an abnormal copy of the *ATP7B* gene from each parent. Carriers of one defective *ATP7B* gene do not have symptoms of Wilson's disease, but their chance of having children with Wilson's disease is increased.

Symptoms can vary widely and some patients may even remain asymptomatic throughout their lifetime. Onset of symptoms can be as varied as the symptoms themselves; new cases have been reported in people as young as 2 and as old as 72, but manifestations typically occur between ages 5 and 35. The most common symptoms of this disease include liver cirrhosis, neurological signs (such as slurred speech), tremors, dystonia (muscle contractions resulting in abnormal postures or positioning of limbs), and psychological manifestations including depression, irrational or bizarre behaviors, loss of focus and/or memory, and problems with controlling emotions.

At the time that I was diagnosed in 1982, the prevalence of Wilson's disease was thought to be extremely rare – 1 out of 200,000 people or 5 people per million. Since then, the numbers have been revised to approximately 1 in 40,000 or 25 per million. Despite being much more common than previously thought, Wilson's disease is still considered a very rare disorder.[3]

---

[3] Note: The number of cases reported by studies in the United States, Europe, and Asia, vary widely with one study reporting incidence as low as 1 in 30,000.

# Chapter 9
## Into the hospital

On the Monday morning following the diagnosis of Wilson's Disease and request to join the research study, my mother and father escorted me to the hospital where I spent the better part of the morning filling out forms and signing disclosures. I was scared, although I didn't show it. I had my own private room, and had brought along books to read and games to play to keep my mind occupied. A nurse took my vital signs, and laid out the plan for the rest of the day. My days to come would be very structured as I went from specialist to specialist and had test after test administered.

\* \* \*

Over the next six weeks, I faced many new challenges, met many new people whose lives I would touch and whose lives would touch mine, underwent countless tests, learned about many diseases and disorders that I never knew existed, but most importantly was used as a vessel by God to share my faith with others in this time of great despair. I witnessed epileptic seizures firsthand and befriended a woman that was a patient in the clinic with St. Vitas Dance. She was a chain smoker and one evening she was smoking on the couch in the lobby, or common area as it was often called. As her cigarette went flying from her fingers and she had rapid involuntary movements of her extremities, it landed between the cushions on the couch and began smoldering; an orderly that was in the area quickly grabbed the nearest fire extinguisher and put out the small fire.

There were many epileptics on the floor but two in particular stick out in my mind. One was a young, bubbly girl, 16 or 17 year-old "Jamie," with blonde hair that was always worn in a ponytail. We often played bumper pool in the common area. One afternoon as we were playing pool with two other patients, Jamie was lining up her cue for a shot when her whole body suddenly sprung rigid and she turned sideways, simultaneously falling. Her head struck the edge of the pool table and she hit the floor shuddering violently. I dropped down on my knees beside her and grabbed her by the shoulders as she jerked and shook with unbelievable strength. Within moments a male and female nurse were over her, trying to restrain her and grasp her tongue. I remember so clearly looking at Jamie and seeing her beautiful brown eyes glazed over and moving convulsively. As quickly as the seizure began, it ended. Jamie lay there, now limp; myself and the two nurses, all spent. I went back to my room, the events reeling through my mind. I sat down on my bed and opened my Bible to the 23rd Psalm...

*"1 The LORD is my shepherd; I shall not want.*

*2 He maketh me to lie down in green pastures: he leadeth me beside the still waters.*

*3 He restoreth my soul: he leadeth me in the paths of righteousness for his name's sake.*

*4 Yea, though I walk through the valley of the shadow of death, I will fear no evil: for thou art with me; thy rod and thy staff they comfort me.*

*5 Thou preparest a table before me in the presence of mine enemies: thou anointest my head with oil; my cup runneth over.*

*6 Surely goodness and mercy shall follow me all the days of my life: and I will dwell in the house of the LORD for ever."*

Another traumatic afternoon in the ward!

\* \* \*

Daniel was another epileptic that I remember well from the 5th floor wing of the neurological disorders research center. Daniel was 19 or 20 and loved to read science fiction books. He was very quiet and shy, but once I got to know him a little, we had great conversations about our respective illnesses. Daniel was always smiling except when he was about to have a seizure; oddly, he could tell when he was going to have a seizure, stating he could feel his head and face get warm and he would feel a sudden onset of a headache. Whenever this occurred, Daniel would head to his room and lay down on his bed very still. That, he said, often miraculously stopped the seizure from occurring, but more importantly, reduced his risk of injury.

\* \* \*

One patient from the wing of the hospital where I resided was Lisa , and she will live on in my heart forever. Lisa was 12 or 13 when I met her. I was 28. She had Metachromatic Leukodystrophy (MLD), a genetic disease that results in muscle wasting. MLD is caused by a deficiency of a specific enzyme. The lack of the lipid metabolizing enzyme results in a buildup of fatty molecules in nerve, liver, and kidney tissues.

Lisa and her family were from Axton, Virginia, and Lisa's parents would stay in a hotel near NIH while she was in the hospital for extended periods of time. Lisa could no longer talk, although she could make sounds. She was in a wheelchair and drooled constantly. The muscles in her neck were too weak to hold her head up.

I would visit Lisa in her room and tell her how pretty she was and make her laugh. Lisa's parents welcomed the attention that I gave Lisa, and her mom told me Lisa's story; that she had been a normal, fun loving girl, cheerleader and  star student at the age of 10. Then, without warning, Lisa was not well. Progression of this horrible disabling disease occurred very rapidly. Lisa's father pulled a picture from his wallet. It was a picture of Lisa in the 5th grade in a little cheerleading uniform. I was blown away! This couldn't be the same Lisa I was facing, the one in a wheelchair, her muscles wasting away. All I could think for the rest of that day was why Lord, why?

I visited Lisa regularly and spoke with her parents often. We talked of our faith and they believed that, whatever the outcome in Lisa's deteriorating situation, God would be glorified.

Lisa was scheduled to be there for 10 days, after which time her parents would be taking her back home. Lisa had a younger sister who was staying with a relative in their hometown so she could remain in school. The morning Lisa was set to leave, I jumped on the elevator and went downstairs to the gift shop. I purchased a vase with a colorful bouquet of flowers and a "Best of luck" card. When I stepped through the doorway of Lisa's room, Lisa let out a shout of joy followed by tears. I bent over and hugged her as I set the fragrant blossoms next to her. She wanted to hold me, but her frail little arms were immobile. Lisa's mom and dad each gave me hugs of gratitude and nurses had gathered around the room and outside in the hall. There were plenty of smiles but not a single dry eye.

Over the next four years, I remained in touch with the Lisa's family and we met and dined out during two of their return visits to NIH. I called them on every holiday and the most difficult part of the call was talking to Lisa. She was very vocal and had a laugh that I cannot describe. I would choke back the tears because I knew she had something to say, but only nonsense sounds came forth. I felt that it was God's plan that our paths had crossed.

Roughly two years after I last visited with Lisa

and her parents over dinner in Bethesda, Maryland (where NIH is located), I called their home in Axton. It was Easter Sunday and Lisa's sister answered the phone; she recognized my voice from previous calls. She didn't have the zing in her voice that I remembered as she said, "I'll get mom." When Lisa's mom answered the phone, I immediately sensed something was really wrong. I asked how everyone was doing and then she answered... "Don died." I could not believe my ears. I said "What?" "Don had an attack of pancreatitis, was life-flighted to the University of North Carolina hospital and died on the operating table," said Lisa's mom. Don was Lisa's father, and I was left speechless. What could I say? What could I do?

Lisa got on the phone and it took nearly all my strength to talk to her. She laughed half heartedly, and I wanted so badly to be there with the her and her family to share in their grief.

I continued to call, and I wrote letters and sent cards to the Lisa and her family. More importantly, I prayed for them. I prayed for peace, understanding, and especially for the healing of Lisa's body.

A year passed and Lisa's mom told me that Lisa's health had deteriorated further. Thanksgiving time rolled around and I called again. Lisa's mom answered, informing me that it was over. Lisa had passed away a few months earlier. Lisa's mom sounded relieved, but I knew it had to be so painful… the loss of her husband and then her daughter. She told me that someday she would be reunited with Lisa and Don… she said God's word assured her of this.

\* \* \*

I had test after test conducted throughout the six weeks I was in NIH. Everything from a liver biopsy to numerous spinal taps. Day in and day out, phlebotomists were drawing blood, and I had to collect my urine around the clock so researchers could monitor how much excess copper my body was eliminating. Doctors and nurses were constantly putting IVs into me, and when the veins in my arms collapsed, they used veins in the back of my hands. Was this payback for the way I had abused the temple of the Lord? I Corinthians 6:19-20 reads,

*19 What? know ye not that your body is the temple of the Holy Ghost which is in you, which ye have of God, and ye are not your own?*
*20 For ye are bought with a price: therefore glorify God in your body, and in your spirit, which are God's.*

Although I don't think so, it was certainly a reminder of what my life could have been like had I chosen to give in to using needles, that one night not so very long ago.

\* \* \*

What would my life be like if my disease had progressed so far that some of the damage was irreversible? Would I not have been better off on the path of destruction that I had headed down just a few years back? I had been on the road to spiritual recovery, but now I felt anger towards God beginning to quell.

\* \* \*

At the end of six weeks, I was discharged from the clinical trial. I had been evaluated and advised by countless specialists: neurologists, hepatologists, gastroenterologists, psychologists, psychiatrists, nutritionists, and social workers. The prognosis (given the rarity of the disease and lack of knowledge coupled with the late onset of symptoms) was not promising. The optimistic doctors gave me a decade if I complied 100% with their instructions. The pessimists gave me three years. At best I wouldn't see 40... worst case, I would die before I reached the age of 30. The bad news was that I had wasted most of my life... the good news was that God had a timeline and a plan for my life, which had been carefully designed by Him and was a mystery to both myself and the medical professionals.

# Chapter 10
## On the Mend

There is nothing more important to maintaining your health than understanding your condition, your treatment options, what your lab results mean, and any new or alternative views on your specific conditions.

After being released from NIH, that is exactly what I did. I ordered the only two books that had been published regarding Wilson's disease. I researched the side effects of the drug that I was given, penacillamine, which acted as a chelator (a chemical compound that binds heavy metals). Penicillamine, a derivative of penicillin, was introduced as an effective pharmacological agent for the treatment of Wilson's disease, and other conditions involving heavy metal toxicity in the body, by Dr. James Walshe, ironically in 1954, the year I was born. Despite the benefits of this medication, Penicillamine can have mild to severe side effects, ranging from loss of appetite and nausea to difficulty breathing and tightness of the chest. Additionally, penicillamine depletes the patient of vitamin B6, which can lead to numerous problems including neurological changes.

Compliance with doctors' prescribed pharmacological therapy alone was not going to reverse the disease that had become a heavy burden on the lives of myself and my parents; adherence to a low copper diet designed by nutritionists was also necessary. I was back in Maryland (the place I consider home) living not far from the Chesapeake Bay, home to the world's best crabs, Maryland blue crabs, and biggest and best oysters, Chincoteague oysters. I love Maryland's seafood; unfortunately, most seafood, shellfish in particular, is very high in copper, and I had to say no to shellfish for the time being. I could go on and on about the sacrifices I had to make where a low copper diet is concerned – no chocolate, bananas, coconut; white meat of chicken or turkey is okay, but not dark… the list goes on and on.

\* \* \*

As the weeks passed, my health began to improve. I put on weight, despite the restrictive diet. My parents and friends noticed changes that I couldn't detect, saying I was much more pleasant to be around and that I had a more positive disposition.

Soon, however, the biggest challenge I was facing was no longer my health condition but meeting the costs of the prescriptions and doctors. Several months, six to be exact, after being discharged from NIH, I needed a prescription refill. Upon my discharge, I was given a six month supply of Cuprimine, the trade name for penicillamine; there was no generic brand. Although penicillamine was also used in the treatment of rheumatoid arthritis, it was considered an orphan drug. An orphan drug is a Food and Drug Administration classification of drugs for medications used to treat diseases that rarely occur (less than 200,000 known cases in the United States) or where is no hope for recovery of development costs. Because there is little financial incentive for the pharmaceutical industry to produce these drugs, orphan drug status gives the manufacturer specific financial incentives to provide the drug. One incentive is no pricing regulation. Coincidentally, or unfortunately depending on how you choose to look at it, the Orphan Drug Act was passed in 1983. That same year that the Act was passed and went into effect, I had to purchase my first prescription of penicillamine.

I was living at home with my parents, working and making a little more than minimum wage. I did not have health insurance and the only insurance options that were affordable to me would exclude the treatment of Wilson's disease. The NIH specialists were still following up on my health; however, they were slowly weaning me from their services. I had no idea how much my "meds," which had to be refrigerated for stability, would cost me. My physician wrote my prescription on a prescription pad. Remember this was 1983. I took the piece of paper which read "Penicillamine 2 x 250 mg TID" scribbled on it with the doctor's illegible signature. TID is medical shorthand for three times per day. The order was for two 250 milligram tablets x three times per day x 30 days or 180 tablets. The cost was unbelievable! $390 for one month's supply!

(Don't misunderstand me. This is not an endorsement for universal healthcare. Just my story!)

\* \* \*

Well, when one allows God to work, amazing things happen. I do not recall specifically how everything fell together and how over the next few years the means were provided for continued doctor visits and the necessary medicine, but I know and believe in the words found in Matthew 6:

*25 Therefore I say unto you, Take no thought for your life, what ye shall eat, or what ye shall drink; nor yet for your body, what ye shall put on. Is not the life more than meat, and the body than raiment?*

*26 Behold the fowls of the air: for they sow not, neither do they reap, nor gather into barns; yet your heavenly Father feedeth them. Are ye not much better than they?*

*27 Which of you by taking thought can add one cubit unto his stature?*

*28 And why take ye thought for raiment? Consider the lilies of the field, how they grow; they toil not, neither do they spin:*

*29 And yet I say unto you, That even Solomon in all his glory was not arrayed like one of these.*

*30 Wherefore, if God so clothe the grass of the field, which to day is, and to morrow is cast into the oven, shall he not much more clothe you, O ye of little faith?*

*31 Therefore take no thought, saying, What shall we eat? or, What shall we drink? or, Wherewithal shall we be clothed?*

*32 (For after all these things do the Gentiles seek:) for your heavenly Father knoweth that ye have need of all these things.*

*33 But seek ye first the kingdom of God, and his righteousness; and all these things shall be added unto you.*

*34 Take therefore no thought for the morrow: for the morrow shall take thought for the things of itself. Sufficient unto the day is the evil thereof.*

In retrospect, the provisions resulted from trusting God... trusting Him as I had done as a small child.

\* \* \*

As my trust for the Lord increased, my health improved and I, along with my parents, thought it was time for me to return to school. I wanted to give back to the medical community, so I enrolled in school full time at Howard Community College in Columbia, Maryland. My parents enjoyed having the "old" Mark back again and welcomed me to stay with them as I pursued my degree.

I loved school, and I did very well maintaining a 4.0 grade point average through my first three semesters. I had a dual major and worked towards degrees in medical technology and secondary education. I completely threw myself into my schoolwork and Dr. Susan Bard, a professor of biology, saw I had great potential. I worked as her lab assistant and excelled in biology and genetics which I found extremely fascinating.

I graduated from Howard Community College in the spring of 1986 with two Associate degrees – Secondary Education and Medical Technology. I was president of the student body and had been appointed in 1985 to the Maryland State Scholarship Board by former Governor Harry Hughes. At the end of my appointment term to the State Board, I was reappointed by the new, incoming governor, William Donald Schaefer. The University of Maryland had accepted me to their School of Education and their School of Chemical and Life Sciences.

I had given God control of my life and I was well on the mend, physically, emotionally, and most importantly, spiritually!

# Chapter 11
## Diagnosing Wilson's disease

How many people go undiagnosed or misdiagnosed with Wilson's disease still remains a mystery. There is case after case, however, of psychiatric patients being misdiagnosed. I would venture to say now, since diagnostic tools are more readily available and knowledge of Wilson's disease has expanded, the number of cases of Wilson's disease that are misdiagnosed is reduced.

Psychiatrists often label cases as "bi-polar disorder" or "attention-deficit disorder" when they lack a clear indication of what the patient actually suffers from based on the symptoms presented, or lack thereof. This might be giving psychiatrists a bad rap, but considering my personal experiences with psychiatrists, I believe that the bad "rap" is not unearned.

Carol Terry is just one example of misdiagnosis. This is an excerpt of her story in the article "Live and let live" written by Berton Roueche in *The New Yorker*, July 16, 1979.

> *Carol Terry began to suffer the symptoms of the disease in 1971, when she was 25, and was treated by psychiatrists in Salt Lake City with drugs such as Thorazine, Valium, L -dopa, and with shock treatment, not to mention inappropriate and aggravating therapy, until, in 1973, Dr. David Reiser, at the Community Mental Health Center, where Mrs. Terry was a welfare patient, recognized Wilson's disease and referred her for testing and to Dr. George E. Cartwright, a specialist on the disease, who treated her and restored most of her functions.*

I met Carol in 1987 at a restaurant in Arlington, Virginia. She is co-founder of the Wilson's Disease Association and a delightful lady. Because her diagnosis came years after the disease had advanced, neurological symptoms weren't totally reversed and she is in a wheelchair.

* * *

Now, mental health is as important as physical health, and I believe that the two are so tightly interwoven that poor mental health leads to poor physical health and vice-versa. I also believe that psychiatry, particularly establishing appropriate pharmaceutical therapy, is more times than not, "hit or miss", and not based on established scientific methodology.

Certainly, Dr. "B" would disagree with me on the latter point. Dr. B was the psychiatric team leader during my hospital stay at UC Davis in 2007, and he and I do not see eye to eye on either my diagnosis or my treatment plan. I believe he is of French descent and he wore a bow tie and lab coat as he made his rounds. From my limited observations, bow ties and lab coats are the typical attire of many "shrinks."

Dr. B thought I should be on Effexor, a drug in the category of selective serotonin and norepinephrine reuptake inhibitors (SSNRIs). Effexor is used to treat major depressive disorder, anxiety, and panic disorder, and works by restoring the balance of natural chemicals in the brain, which helps to improve certain mood problems. I had been given Lexapro, an SSRI (selective serotonin reuptake inhibitor), a couple of years before when I broke down crying in Dr. Rossaro's office a few years back. That had been a horrible experience, because I was suicidal before nightfall of the first day taking Lexapro.

I had researched the various antidepressants, although I didn't even want to be on any antidepressants, but Dr. B insisted I try Effexor. Sure enough, as much of the literature suggests, I became suicidal again as a result of taking the antidepressant and slipped into a deep depression within 48 hours of starting the medication.

\* \* \*

My purpose is not to indict all doctors, psychiatrists or psychologists. I truly believe that doctors, including Dr. B, have their patients' best interests in mind. I also feel that doctors work long hours under a lot of stress, and mistakes and wrong diagnoses are bound to happen. Think about the stress factor... doctors literally are responsible for their patients' lives. They are responsible for looking at all aspects of their patients' lives and how and which factors play into disease and wellness. That is why patient history and family histories are so vital and physicians need to know all about your personal life.

Take, for instance, accidents. As I mentioned previously, my parents always said I was accident-prone and I have certainly had my fair share. Whether the accidents I have had are directly or indirectly related to my Wilson's disease, I may never know. Perhaps some graduate student or researcher sitting in an obscure basement at the University of Siberia may draw some type of correlation while reviewing my vast medical file compiled over the past 55 years.

Where do I begin and what do I include? If you look at all the accidents that I have had or been in, I would have to write a separate series with three complete volumes: Volume 1 - Unavoidable accidents; Volume 2 - Avoidable accidents resulting from bad decisions; Volume 3 - Avoidable accidents resulting from stupid, stupid things I did.

My better judgment tells me to not bore you with the details. Just understand that being accident prone could be directly related to lack of coordination or neurological problems coupled with poor judgment (All of which could be Wilson's disease related).

# Chapter 12
## First Marriage

Speaking of accidents...
My first marriage, 1990 - 1997... was a real train wreck!
Enough said... Next!

# Chapter 13
## Back to California

In 1988, my mother retired from Sears, my father's health had deteriorated, and they had decided to move to Northern California, closer to my sister Cathy. I stayed behind in Laurel, Maryland to continue my education which was becoming increasingly difficult. I was working full-time and attending school part-time.

Two years passed, and a gut-feeling told me that I needed to be closer to my parents. My dad was only 69 years old, but I felt he would not be with us much longer. I moved to Elk Grove, California and went to work at an industrial chemical development plant. I was working in the lab by Arco Arena on a Saturday, March 16, 1991 to be exact, when I got a call that my father had been rushed to Methodist hospital after a massive heart attack.

I arrived at the hospital in 30 short minutes, it

seemed like it took hours. My dad was in a coma. We would never have another conversation again, that is, in this life. On Tuesday, March 19th, my mother, sister Cathy, and I gathered at mama and daddy's home, to call my sister JoAnne. The four of us made the decision that we would have him taken off of life support the following day. We knew that was his wish.

At 11:50 that same evening, the Lord took the decision from us and welcomed my daddy into His arms.

# Chapter 14
## Visit to Dr. Brewer's Clinic

B y 1992, my compliance with taking the Cupramine was very poor. There were a couple of reasons for this: I had once again become very forgetful, my body was becoming less tolerant of the heavy metal chelating agent, and I experienced tremendous abdominal pains. Dr. George Brewer of the University of Michigan was conducting clinical trials on the efficacy of zinc sulfate in the treatment of Wilson's disease, so I inquired further as to how to become a research participant.

As research had continued on penicillamine, the treatment of choice, newer studies had indicated that penicillamine could lead to toxic levels of free copper. Apparently, penicillamine can release copper bound up by the protein metallothionein and store the unbound copper in the liver.

Dr. Brewer's research on zinc was very promising and the cost of zinc, which could be purchased over the counter for about $8.00 for a month's supply, was very attractive. The key was finding out how I would respond to zinc therapy.

My sister Cathy has always been very charitable. After discussions with her husband, Eric, they offered to buy me a round trip ticket to Ann Arbor, Michigan.

Dr. Brewer needed me in the research hospital for one full week to conduct tests and observations. I my mind, there was no fear like I had experienced a decade earlier. I knew what was wrong, I recognized that my body was no longer responding to the penicillamine well, and most of all, I recognized that this was God's hand reaching out to me again and saying, "trust Me, you belong to Me."

I flew to Ann Arbor, Michigan early on a Friday in the late spring of 1982 to check in to the research hospital at the University of Michigan. After I settled into my hospital room, Dr. Brewer came to my room, introduced himself, and chatted with me about the protocol for the following week. I had become accustomed to being a human "subject" and felt that even if this "new" treatment wasn't effective for me, the data gathered from my case could provide answers to questions that Dr.

Brewer was proposing. Someone was bound to benefit, and that was a good thing!

When I returned to California, I had a renewed faith and a new treatment plan. Dr. Paul Seites, the physician that stood by me and my family as my father's physician, had moved over to the U.C. Davis Medical Group and was now managing my health. My life had extended beyond NIH's most optimistic doctors' predictions.

# Chapter 15
## The Best Was Yet to Come

Nothing significant occurred between 1992 and 1997. I responded well to the zinc and maintained a healthy life, relative to the past. My first marriage ended in 1996, and the divorce was finalized 1997. That same year, I got my real estate license.

I was discouraged by the termination of my first marriage, an institution that is ordained and sanctified by God. On the other hand, as strange as this may sound, it now seems that my first marriage was a part of God's plan to unite me with my one true soul mate, a woman as beautiful as her name... Zeta!

The circumstances which surrounded my meeting Zeta were unusual for the time. Internet dating wasn't what it is today. People might meet on-line, but on-line dating services had not yet evolved.    I started chatting with Zeta in a Sacramento chat room.   We spent a few evenings "instant messaging" each other and basically flirting.  I told her that I was 42 and didn't have any children; she said she wouldn't date anyone over 40 and she was interested in someone that had children, so they would be prepared to deal with her three.  I knew God had given me the desire to be a father and my dad had been a great role model of both a good husband and good father.

I was thirteen years older than Zeta and I had no children.   I had been completely honest as God would have me be.  I wasn't sure what His plan was in this situation, but I knew what I wanted, so I was persistent.

My persistence paid off and Zeta agreed to go out with me.  Love at first sight... for me at least!  I knew I didn't want to live my life alone and she was beautiful, intelligent, and had three lovely children. We first met for breakfast on a Friday morning, January 10, 1997, at Carrow's Restaurant on "J" Street in Sacramento; I had originally asked her out on a first date for Saturday night, the 11th, but was so anxious to meet her that I just couldn't wait that long.  A third wheel tagged along, but one that I welcomed: Lyndsie, her beautiful daughter, now my daughter too and the "apple of my eye!".  Lyndsie was four at the time, and before breakfast was finished, she was crawling all over me.

That afternoon, Zeta invited me over to her apartment. I met Steven and A.J., my two boys, and I sat down on the couch, put my arm around Zeta and told her that I wasn't looking for short-term love. She said, "That's fine, but I plan to date other guys." I quickly retorted, "Go right ahead. I'm going to sweep you off your feet!" I was cocky, a trait she admits attracted her to me.

My intentions were to marry Zeta, and although, my Wilson's disease was, at the time, well under control, I knew it would be wrong to conceal my condition.

A few weeks after we had begun dating, I sat down with Zeta and told her that I had something I needed to tell her. Later, she would confess, that she thought I was going to tell her I was an alcoholic or drug addict. I told Zeta of my Wilson's disease and what it could mean in the "big picture" of things. Three months later, I asked Zeta to marry me. As I recall, she didn't hesitate before saying "YES!"

We were married on the south steps of the California State Capitol Building on November 8, 1997. I recmember that it was the last sunny Saturday of the year and the sunny days that were to follow for Zeta, myself, and our three children, would far outnumber the cloudy ones. God had "done real good" in finding a wife for me.

Zeta was saved shortly after we married. We placed church membership at Cypress Missionary Baptist Church where we remain members to this day. Steven accepted the gift of Salvation the following year, and two weeks later, AJ accepted Christ. On Father's day in 2003, Lyndsie knocked on Zeta's and my bedroom door and said that she wanted Christ to live in her. That has to be the best Father's day gift of all time!

The Lord has been very good to me and my family, and He continues to amaze me by showing how much He cares for me.

# Chapter 16
## An Angel Appears

Because of the cirrhotic condition of my liver due to copper toxicity, I am required to have regular lab workups, MRIs, CAT scans, and ultrasounds. In 2003, I was referred by Dr. Seites to a gastroenterologist for follow up. That is when I met Dr. Valentina Medici, a brilliant doctor with a bedside manner and heart of the late Mother Teresa. She is truly an angel!

Dr. Medici's research focuses on the molecular biochemistry of Wilson's disease. She is gentle, thorough, and very caring. Any patient of Dr. Medici should consider themselves blessed.

On my visit, Dr. Medici surprised me when she gave me her cell phone number and said, "If you need to reach me, here is my number." Little did I know that five years later, that number would save me from my own self destruction.

\* \* \*

By the time I met Dr. Medici, I had been on Zinc therapy for a little over 10 years. She had been conducting research on the efficacy of the drug Trientine in treating Wilson's disease patients. I had become intolerant of zinc, regardless of the form - zinc sulfate, zinc acetate, or zinc gluconate - so I was a perfect candidate for Trientine therapy.

Dr. Medici, as I said, was thorough and she had me seeing Dr. Vicki Wheelock, a neurologist, along with other specialists, and she was communicating thoroughly with them about my health!

Over the next several years, I was back on track to feeling well with Trientine. I saw Dr. Medici on a regular basis, and whenever I had other issues, knee surgeries, heart catherization, or hospitalized for any reason, Dr. Medici would follow up.

I recall one routine visit to see Dr. Medici a little more than one year ago. I had spoken a few weeks prior with Dr. Wheelock about how I might go about donating my body for research. After all, I thought, surely doctors and scientists could benefit from examining my diseased liver and brain. When I approached Dr. Medici with the idea, she appeared to be taken aback. Puzzled by her reaction but wanting to know, I appealed to her, "Can you tell me how to go about donating my body for Wilson's disease research?" She answered emphatically, "No!" Now knowing that cadavers are valuable for research, I continued my query, "Well, why not?" Her response came in a most caring tone, "Because I only want to think of you alive."

About six months later I received an email from Dr. Medici; the email contained several contacts with regards to donating my body to science.

\* \* \*

I had returned to school in 2005 and completed my baccalaureate degree at California State University, Sacramento (CSUS), in the Summer of 2006. I immediately entered a master's program through the University of Maryland, researching sea lions in the Sacramento delta. My research was conducted in conjunction with CSUS and in the spring of 2006, with my data collected and my thesis near complete, I enrolled in a marine ecology class at San Francisco State University. I traveled to Sausalito, California every Monday morning for the marine ecology class. Maybe, I was overdoing it, that is a possibility, but my depression and suicidal thoughts had begun to resurface and I may have been attempting to distract myself.

One sunny Monday in early May, I had the top down on my Chrysler Sebring convertible. Driving towards Vallejo singing along with "Billy Joel's Greatest Hits," the volume cranked up and belting out lyrics at the top of my lungs, I was struck with an urge, a horrifying urge to turn the steering wheel and slam into the concrete barrier in the median strip. I looked at my speedometer. 75 miles per hour! I resisted. I took my foot off the gas and pulled over to the shoulder of the road and collected myself. I took the HealthNet insurance card out of my wallet and, using my cell phone, called the 800 number on the back. The operator said she would get a nurse on the line. The sound of the nurse's voice gave me a calm and she was able to talk me down – an unknown angel!

I met with a psychologist twice a week over the next few weeks. Talking helped, but I was still experiencing disturbing thoughts of suicidal ideation. I had not shared this with Zeta and I was unsure how to.

\* \* \*

It was mid May, 2008. The Sunday prior, I had come close to suicide at the railroad tracks. I was feeling really depressed and experiencing great difficulty. I tried to mask my feelings from everyone, but my wife could sense that something was wrong. We had an argument the day before, and Zeta knew that I was struggling.

I insisted Zeta go to church, telling her that I would come for services at 11:00 a.m. The time was 9:40 in the morning and Zeta left with Lyndsie. A.J., who plays in the praise band, was already at church, and Steven was living in San Diego.

I went upstairs to my office and pulled up the Google search engine. As my eyes began to well up with tears, I typed in "how do children cope with parent suicide". I hit enter. The search results came up. I quickly scanned them and then I glanced away from the screen. My eyes were so watery, I could not focus. I looked down at the floor and there, lying underneath the desk, was a piece of paper that had been given to me five years prior and was now old and yellowed by sun exposure; it was Dr. Medici's cell phone number.

I picked it up and began to dial the number. Dr. Medici answered on the second ring. "Hello." I was totally in tears by then. I choked out the words through my tears, "Dr. Medici…. I'm in trouble…" She recognized my voice even through the tears. "Mark, what's wrong?" "I don't want to live anymore," I managed to say. "Where are you?" she said, "where is your wife?" Her voice began to calm me. I told her that Zeta had gone to church and I was home alone. She asked for Zeta's cell number, but before I could tell her, I heard the door open downstairs. Zeta ran up the stairs and into the office; I handed her the phone. The next thing I remember was Zeta taking me to the U.C. Davis emergency room where Dr. Medici had two physicians, familiar with Wilson's disease, waiting to admit me. Many angels were watching out for me that day!

# Chapter 17
## Still Here

I am still here thanks to all that love and care that others have given me. I feel especially indebted to Dr. Medici and her attention to every meticulous detail of my health for which I am both grateful and perplexed.

After being hospitalized in May of 2006, I was put on Celexa or citalopram. Celexa is an SSRI similar to Lexapro. I really struggled with taking an antidepressant, but a new psychiatrist was managing my case and adjusted the dosage very gradually. I was able to focus much better and I completed my master's degree in life sciences in August of 2008. I was hired to teach biology and natural resource management courses at American River College following the conferring of my degree. Dr. Medici has presented her research to three of my general biology classes. She is very articulate and the students appreciate her presentations and her knowledge of copper metabolism.

I continued treatment with Celexa for almost a year, but felt "numb" most of the time. That is the best way to describe Celexa's effect on me... it "numbed me". My relationship with my wife and children began to deteriorate, and I began to withdraw altogether.

I am no longer on any antidepressant; I try to eat healthier and exercise more often, remembering that a healthy lifestyle generally leads to better mental health.

I will be 56 this year. Doctors didn't expect me to live beyond 30 or 35. I recognize that God still has some grand purpose that has not yet been fulfilled in my life, because I am still here!

I have begun working on my doctorate in psychology... now, how crazy is that? I hope to someday provide some answers to questions regarding depression in Wilson's disease. You see, I believe that I have often been misunderstood by others, others that do not recognize, realize, or understand the many psychological ramifications of a condition such as Wilson's disease. I find myself constantly seeking encouragement, yet hardly appreciating support other than that which is provided by my immediate family.

In order to keep going, I have realized not to

depend on others for encouragement. Being in God's Word daily has a far greater effect than man can have in that regard. I also have a poem that hangs on my office wall that keeps me encouraged:

## Don't Quit

*When things go wrong as they sometimes will,*
*When the road you're trudging seems all up hill,*
*When the funds are low and the debts are high*
*And you want to smile, but you have to sigh,*
*When care is pressing you down a bit,*
*Rest if you must, but don't you quit.*
*Life is queer with its twists and turns,*
*As every one of us sometimes learns,*
*And many a failure turns about*
*When he might have won had he stuck it out;*
*Don't give up though the pace seems slow—*
*You may succeed with another blow,*
*Often the goal is nearer than it seems to a faint and faltering man;*
*Often the struggler has given up when he might have captured the victor's cup;*
*And he learned too late when the night came down,*
*How close he was to the golden crown.*

*Success is failure turned inside out—*
*The silver tint of the clouds of doubt,*
*And you never can tell how close you are,*
*It may be near when it seems so far;*
*So stick to the fight when you're hardest hit—*
*It's when things seem worst that you must not quit.*

-Edgar A. Guest -

# Final Chapter
## The Bucket List

I took my wife, Zeta, on a date[4] to see the movie "The Bucket List." The movie, starring Morgan Freeman and Jack Nicholson, came out in 2007. The story is about two men from two very different backgrounds who have one thing in common – they were both terminally ill. They leave the hospital together to do the things they wanted to do before they die, crossing thing off of their "bucket list".

I have been fortunate enough to do many things in my lifetime. I have traveled to six other countries, visited 47 of the 50 states, been scuba diving and sky diving; I have flown a Bellanca Viking over the Sutter Buttes and a Cessna over the Golden Gate

---

[4] Note to married men: Dating your wife can keep your marriage healthy. Take her to dinner, the movies, the theater… just take her out. You will be surprised what that will do for your marriage!

Bridge. I have kayaked the flat water of the American River and rafted the white water of the Youghiogheny River. I have sailed in the Chesapeake Bay as well as the Caribbean and watched the sun rise and set on exotic islands. I have attended Easter Sunday Service in the little chapel in what John Muir considered the greatest cathedral of all, the Yosemite Valley. So for me to want to do more seems quite selfish. After all, God has given me many more years than the doctors' best estimates.

Nevertheless, I feel it quite fitting to conclude my story with my "Bucket List". It is presented in the same order it was written more than a year ago – with one crossed out.

1. Hold a Rwandan orphan.
2. Sail San Francisco Bay.
3. Visit Yellowstone National Park.
4. Climb Half Dome.
5. Ride a "century". (100-mile bike ride)
6. See the Tour de France "live".
7. Own another cabin cruiser.
8. Go fishing for marlin in Cabo.
9. ~~Finish writing my book~~.
10. Own another corvette.

# Afterword

This book was written by me, and I have done my very best to give factual information, but that is not what is important. Although this is my story, the story is not meant to be just about me. This story is about the relationship that the Father has had with me since I accepted Jesus Christ as my personal Savior, and in doing so, became a child of God.

Through bad times and good times, through highs and lows, through thick and thin, He has been there, waiting and watching, and hoping that my relationship with Him would be the most important relationship to me in my life.

The prophet Isaiah said, speaking of Christ, the Messiah, in chapter 53, verse 5:

*"But he was wounded for our transgressions, he was bruised for our iniquities: the chastisement of our peace was upon him; and with his stripes we are healed."*

Why would I, a child of God, allow Satan to rule over me? I did... there is no denying it and someday I will stand before God, from whom there was no hiding my sins. Remember in the opening chapter of this book, when I sat at the railroad tracks on the verge of suicide and Satan was urging me with just another one of his lies, "No one else will be hurt!" Satan lost that battle of my mind, and I believe God has turned that victory on Satan, that through His use of this story to reach others, perhaps "Many will be saved!"

Finally, I would be remiss if I failed to mention the role my earthly parents played in the strengthening of my faith. My mother and father knew the struggles of growing up; after all, they were once young too. My father in the 36 years I knew him was a great role model of a loving father and a loving husband. My mother provided plenty of nurturing and still does at age 84. They both believed strongly in the words written in Proverbs 22:6 -

*"Train up a child in the way he should go: and when he is old, he will not depart from it."*

I am living, breathing proof of that scripture.

And my dad also took stock of Proverbs 13:24 on numerous occasions.

*"He that spareth his rod hateth his son: but he that loveth him chasteneth him betimes."*

My father was so certain of his investment as a parent, he wrote a letter to my mom that she later found. In it he wrote:

*"Try to stay close to Mark, he can help you so much."*

\* \* \*

I hope that through this true story of my life that perhaps God's plan for you and His desire to have a relationship with you will be revealed.

I recognize God every day, and because of my great interest in the natural world, I see Him and the glory of His works. As the Psalmist David says in Psalm 19:1 –

*"The heavens declare the glory of God; and the firmament sheweth his handywork."*

Every opportunity I have to gaze at the moon, I

do. The moon speaks to me, not literally, but I am amazed by how the laws of nature put into place by God operate with such precision. As a scientist, I see His handiwork all about me, and I am in awe.

Scientists, looking on the molecular level have found many reactions that occur in a "domino effect". When I look at these molecular cascades, one triggering the next, I see my Creator in action. In my case, I see the cascade effect of Wilson's disease as a way to bring me back to Him.

# For More Information

There are many sources of Wilson disease information. Some are reliable while others are not. If you are interested in finding out more about Wilson disease, I have listed several reliable sources.

## Organizations:

**Wilson Disease Association**
1802 Brookside Drive
Wooster, OH   44691
info@wilsonsdisease.org
http://www.wilsonsdisease.org
Tel: 330-264-1450 888-264-1450
Fax: 330-264-0974

**American Liver Foundation**
75 Maiden Lane
Suite 603
New York, NY   10038-4810
info@liverfoundation.org
http://www.liverfoundation.org
Tel: 800-GO LIVER (465-4837) 212-668-1000
Fax: 212-483-8179

**Genetic and Rare Diseases (GARD) Information Center**
PO Box 8126
Gaithersburg MD 20898-8126
http://rarediseases.info.nih.gov/Default.aspx
ordr@od.nih.gov
Tel: 301-251-4925  888-205-2311

**March of Dimes**
1275 Mamaroneck Avenue
White Plains, NY   10605
askus@marchofdimes.com
http://www.marchofdimes.com
Tel: 914-997-4488 888-MODIMES (663-4637)
Fax: 914-428-8203

**National Institute of Diabetes and Digestive and Kidney Diseases (NIDDK)**
National Institutes of Health, DHHS
31 Center Drive, Rm. 9A06 MSC 2560
Bethesda, MD   20892-2560
http://www.niddk.nih.gov
Tel: 301-496-3583 TTY: 866-569-1162

**WE MOVE (Worldwide Education & Awareness for Movement Disorders)**
204 West 84th Street
New York, NY   10024
wemove@wemove.org
http://www.wemove.org
Tel: 212-875-8312
Fax: 212-875-8389

## Websites:

www.ninds.nih.gov/disorders/wilsons/wilsons.htm

www.healthline.com/galecontent/wilson-disease-3

www.mayoclinic.org/wilsons-disease/

www.wrongdiagnosis.com/w/wilsons_disease/intro.htm

## Support Groups:

www.inspire.com/groups/wilson-disease-association/

www.mdjunction.com/wilsons-disease

www.wilsonsdisease.org.uk

## Books:

**Wilson's Disease for the Patient and Family: A Patient's Guide to Wilson's Disease and Frequently Asked Questions about Copper (Paperback)**
Author: George Brewer, M.D.

**ISBN-10:** 1401029043
**ISBN-13:** 978-1401029043

**Wilson's Disease: A Clinician's Guide to Recognition, Diagnosis, and Management (Hardcover)**
Author: George Brewer, M.D.

**ISBN-10:** 0792373545
**ISBN-13:** 978-0792373544

Made in the USA
Lexington, KY
09 April 2010